"... *sometimes I know so well what I want.*
... in a picture I want to say something comforting,
as music is comforting.
I want to paint ... with that something of the eternal
which the halo used to symbolize..."

Sunflowers
for
Van Gogh

Sunflowers
for
Van Gogh

David Douglas Duncan

RIZZOLI
NEW YORK

Photography—Text—Design—Production
David Douglas Duncan

Typography Consultant
David Blumenthal
Henry Wolf Productions/New York

Printing & Binding
Dai Nippon Japan

First published in the
United States of America in 1986 by
Rizzoli International Publications, Inc.
597 Fifth Avenue, New York, NY 10017

First edition

ISBN 0-8478-0764-9   LC 86-42729

Title page   Van Gogh   Self-portrait   Paris, 1888
The Metropolitan Museum of Art, New York

All Van Gogh quotations are from
"The Complete Letters of Vincent van Gogh"
New York Graphic Society, 1958

Contents

Paris 1888   Self-portrait   *Rijksmuseum Vincent van Gogh Amsterdam*

Dedicated to Vincent van Gogh
and
Sunflowers
whose short lives he immortalized
together with his own

". . . looking at the stars always makes me dream,
as simply as I dream over the black dots
representing towns and villages on a map.
Why, I ask myself, shouldn't the shining dots of the sky
be as accessible as the black dots on the map of France?
Just as we take the train to Tarascon or Rouen,
we take death to reach a star . . . .

"To die quietly of old age would be to go there on foot."

*Vincent van Gogh and I fell in love in the same way, in the same place,
with the same girl—one hundred years apart. We both knew her only by
her first name. Sunflower.*

*He died when thirty-seven, at the beginning of one of the most passionate,
prolific and already fulfilled lives in a painter's world. Friends of the
artist encircled his coffin with his canvases—a riotous garden of
blues, crimson, emerald and sunburst yellow, blinding yellow so pure
and unfiltered and straight from the squeezed tube and wrenched soul that
nothing lay between Vincent and his God . . . nor his love: Sunflower.
Then they buried him. With the bullet and his vision next to his heart.
Sunflower and Van Gogh soon became synonymous, wedded forever following
a romance now enshrined in millions of hearts where it shares the almost
legendary role of that other celestial tragedy: Romeo and Juliet.*

Preface

Six years ago, while visiting a Dutch friend who had printed several of
my books and later retired to a village within sight of the French Pyrenees,
I saw parched fields of dead sunflowers embracing a long-abandoned windmill.
It reminded me of a Van Gogh painting. I promised myself to return one day
when the flowers would be in bloom. But then I got involved with a book
commemorating Pablo Picasso's birth, another on the Moslem world and one
about a New York street peddler who had taught himself to achieve lofty
heights as a master photographer of the city he might have hated. I only
returned last year. It was mid-summer. Sunflowers were everywhere and in
full bloom, with noontime temperatures around 120 degrees Fahrenheit
and no shade. I shot the windmill and its sunflowers *(pages 48–49)*, then
waded shoulder-deep into other caldrons of molten gold beckoning nearby—
and began to work.

Surprises constantly confronted me while photographing in the same fields
which I had assumed inspired Van Gogh to paint his celebrated sunflowers
nearly a century before I stood braced against the wind in the mistral-
swept valleys of Provence. Those canvases are now so sentimentally priceless
not one owner would loan a sunflower painting to the curators of the mighty
Metropolitan Museum of Art in New York for the 1984 first-ever exhibit of
"Van Gogh in Arles." The same Met that has been loaned everything including
Leonardo da Vinci's *Mona Lisa*. But not one *Sunflower*. My belated research
then revealed that Van Gogh produced just twelve paintings of sunflowers
(I'd always thought there were dozens). There was an almost forgotten bouquet
(today in Mannheim, Germany); then suddenly four dramatic still lifes appeared
of cut blossoms (one in the Metropolitan itself, *page 137*), all painted in
Paris. It was only later, in Arles, that his love for "rustic" sunflowers perhaps
became the inspiration that justified his unrewarded work, while his canvases
were devotional offerings of a private religion. He painted seven sunflower
masterpieces that made him a legend even as he died. Yet he had sold but a
single picture in his life, to the sister of a friend.

Tragically, one of his fanatically protected paintings from Arles, *Sunflowers and Vase with Blue Background* (three of his sunflowers have chartreuse or lemon backgrounds) was destroyed in Yokohama during the Second World War *(page 134)*. So now there are six. There is no Van Gogh of the horizon-to-horizon sunflowers that I saw in such profusion while crisscrossing France for this book. And one morning I understood. In Van Gogh's time sunflowers must have been a rare but sometimes encountered semi-exotic plant, much like tree orchids in Florida when I was a university zoology student roaming the Everglades before the war. Today, sunflowers are commonplace, the source of the greatest commercial vegetable oil crop in Europe, eclipsing olive, peanut, corn oil and everything else. New fields are now being planted everywhere, especially across the French sunbelt—Provence to the Atlantic Coast—where these photographs were taken. Had Van Gogh only seen what I saw last summer he surely would have painted canvases still unimagined.

Those vast flowerscapes are now so familiar to Continental motorists they have sired an amusing paradox in human behavior. During July and August when the sunflower pageant is awesome, millions of Europeans pour into the road networks that lead to Mediterranean, Atlantic Ocean and Spanish beaches. Scandinavian, Japanese, American and other tourists join the exodus of cars and trailers and buses on the autoroutes as everyone heads for the sun. When home again, vacations finished, tens of thousands of them will then wait patiently in line when paintings by Van Gogh are exhibited, the majority apparently anticipating at least a glimpse of one of his *Sunflowers*. Yet, from the middle of last July until almost the middle of August while shooting the sunflowers in this book, I never saw a car stop beside what was perhaps one of the most spirit-lifting floral extravaganzas in the entire world.

And like snowflakes, every sunflower is unique—different from all others.

But not another person pointed a camera at a single blossom.

Even before learning that Van Gogh's total output of *Sunflowers* would cover only a few walls of a modest home; even before watching what appeared to be most of Europe hurtle past shimmering galaxies of sunflowers without stopping in wonderment, I discovered something so funny, outrageous and debunking of a superstar of folklore that I almost hesitate, now, to suggest that one of the most sacred rites in Nature watching is based on fiction. The truth is that *sunflowers do not turn with the sun*. They greet each day facing east, bask in the noonday sun still looking east and warm their back petals against the setting sun *(page 13)*. And I found only four places where I saw exceptions during my entire sunflower safari. I have given them seven pages in this homage to Van Gogh, who might have admired the independence of the loners *(pages 7, 48–49, 116–117 which is the same flower as page 7, 122)* and shared the feeling of terror of those sunflowers who possibly felt they were doomed *(page 83)*.

As for those millions upon millions of others seen during my journey, I can offer one observation as a flat statement of fact. Sunflowers of France never turn, not even for the sun itself—their godfather.

Turning or not turning, mine was a love affair at first sight.

I was out in the fields alone, surrounded by sunflowers who nodded every-where then looked at me coyly-innocently-brazenly-shyly-flirtatiously-tomboyishly-even matronly (that made me laugh because I was older) and then touched my hand while we were bending low together trying to shield each other against the onslaught of the mistral that screeched around us from out of nowhere, slamming us into the ground as I tried to steady a camera, but far worse, it tore at the sunflowers' heads while snatching away whole fistfuls of petals from around their faces which infuriated me as I watched through wind-lashed tears of frustrated rage because I saw my battered companions as girls—and friends.

Vincent van Gogh would have understood, perfectly.

"There is an art of the future,
and it is going to be so lovely
and so young
that even if we give up our youth for it,
we must gain in serenity by it"

Vincent writing to Theo, his brother
Arles, France
May, 1888

Everyone Ignored the Sunflowers

A Mid-Summer's Journey Across France

Provence

XVIII th-century farmhouse
Mountain of the Lubéron

Afternoon   *Medieval village of Lacoste*

It's a Myth—Sunflowers Don't Turn With the Sun

⟨ *Morning-Midday* ⟩

Hilltown of Bonnieux
Valley of the Lubéron

Valley
of the
Lubéron

Violet shadows and glare   *Sirocco dust from Africa*

July in a Sunflower Valley

The
Furnace
Flames of August

High Noon
Over
Provence

"The Devil Mistral"

Provence was a battlefield for Van Gogh, who painted
in the relentless wind and suffocating heat
that dominate all life where sunflowers bloom

Sunflowers of Provence Still Mourn a Friend Named Vincent

Homage
by
Old Sunflowers
to
Van Gogh

The
Monks
of
Arles

Midi-Pyrenees

Holidaying Europeans
had no time for sunflowers
which were found in their fields
spending the summer alone

Noble Fortress
in a
Sunflower Sea

The Roman ramparts
Walled city of Carcassonne

A
Storm
of
Storms
Became Dawn

Fingerprints
in
Gold
Blessed
Our Earth

Then
Night Again
Hid
The Splendor

Discovering
Another World
in
Madeleine's Garden

Home of Mlle Madeleine Gederd   *Village of Duras*

Kids as Knights in Armor

Mothers
and
Children

Vamps

Virgins

Jesters
and
Giants

Madeleine's Tiny Garden Was a Magical Place
For Twenty-five Days
While Her Sunflowers Were in Bloom

Summer's End

Awaiting Destiny
Elderly Faces Veiled in Lace—Amber—Gold

The
Optimist
and
His Fate

of Gentle Lives

flowers in the Pyrenees

*And God
set them
in the firmament
of the heaven
to give light
upon
the earth*

Genesis 1:17

Valley
of
the
Loire

Historic Domaine
of
Kings and Queens
of
France

Yesterday and Tomorrow

Ghosts of Ancient and Future Sovereigns

Château de Chambord   *Loire River nuclear reactors*

Unnoticed panic grips neighbors of the deadly atom
with the cause of their hysteria plainly visible nearby

"Free"
Sunflowers
Face East

Sunup among normal sunflowers
untroubled by atomic reactors

Invaders
from
an
Unknown Star

The lone survivor
A field of onions

Earth's
Daily Theater
at
Nightfall

Sunflowers hiding in mist
Daybreak on the Loire River

A
Medieval
Tapestry
of
Sunflowers

Château de Saumur
Dawn above Loire River

Atlantic Coast

Final Days
of
Glory
of a
Dying Summer

Everyone was at the beach
Sunflowers flank many roads

Another
Storm
Sunrise
and
Journey's End

Gironde estuary at Royan
Cloudburst over the Atlantic

102

Hidden
Fisherman
in a
Valley of Gold

Stealth and silence to no avail
Not a nibble all morning long

The
Harvest Wind
of
Summer

Imagine!
Falling in Love
with a
Sunflower
who
Sought the Wind
and
Shunned the World

*All sunflowers but one face east
Westerly winds from Atlantic Ocean*

His Eyes Menaced a Stranger from Afar

Someone with Fantasy
—a Child or Perhaps a local Picasso—
had Created a Shepherd King
as Protector of All the Sunflowers

Morning—Noon—Night
Sunflowers
Ignore
The Atlantic Ocean

Midday near Royan
Fishing nets on Gironde estuary

Just a Wayside Bouquet
Overflowing with Tranquility
Clover
and
Sunflowers Loved by Someone as Flowers

Vincent Willem van Gogh

Groot-Zundert   Auvers-sur-Oise
Holland   France
30 March 1853   29 July 1890

Your
Sunflowers
Will Live
Forever

GREAT BRITAIN

NORTH SEA

NETHERLANDS

Groot-Zundert

BELGIUM

Lille

ENGLISH CHANNEL

0 ————— 100 miles
0 ————— 100 kilometers

LUX.

WEST GERMANY

Cherbourg   Le Havre

Auvers-sur-Oise

★ Paris

Brest

F R A N C E

Orleans

Chambord

Tours

ATLANTIC COAST

LOIRE VALLEY

Loire R.

Zürich

SWITZERLAND

Geneva

ATLANTIC OCEAN

La Rochelle

Royan

Gironde

Bordeaux

Duras

Rhône R.

Lyons

PROVENCE

ITALY

Lacoste
Lubéron
Avignon
Bonnieux

MONACO

Arles

Nice

Biarritz

MIDI-PYRENEES

Toulouse

Marseilles

Cannes

Carcassonne

Narbonne

SPAIN

ANDORRA

MEDITERRANEAN SEA

A Sunflower Map of France

Paul J. Pugliese

The
Sunflowers
of
Van Gogh

Arles August 1888   *oil on panel*   *Yokohama 1945*

The destroyed "Sunflowers"

Paris Autumn 1886   oil on canvas   The first sunflowers   *Kunsthalle Mannheim*
50.5 × 61.5 (19⁷/₈ × 24¹/₂)

Sunflowers and Van Gogh have been as one word in the art-and-street vocabulary of beauty for nearly a century. Yet he painted only twelve sunflower pictures, five in Paris and seven when he moved to Arles in Provence. So it is strange, in view of the Van Gogh-sunflower mystique, that this book-appendix catalogue raisonné apparently is the only place where they may be seen together, alone, and in color. After such adulation of the artist and his favorite subject that's difficult to understand.

On December 24, 1888, Van Gogh mutilated himself almost fatally when he hit a vein while amputating part of his ear. He still gift-wrapped the fragment as a surprise for a friend in a nearby bordello of Arles— Merry Christmas! She fainted. The next day Theo, Vincent's adored art-dealer brother in Paris arrived at the hospital accompanied by Paul Gauguin who had been living and painting with Van Gogh for several tumultuous months in his little "Yellow House," the studio-home Van Gogh had dreamed of as a center for painters who would come to Arles to escape the politics-in-art of Paris. *(continued on page 138)*

Paris Autumn 1887   oil on canvas   Rijksmuseum Vincent van Gogh Amsterdam
20.5 × 26.5 (8¹/₈ × 10¹/₂)

Paris Autumn 1887   oil on canvas   Kunstmuseum Bern
50 × 60 (19³/₄ × 23⁵/₈)

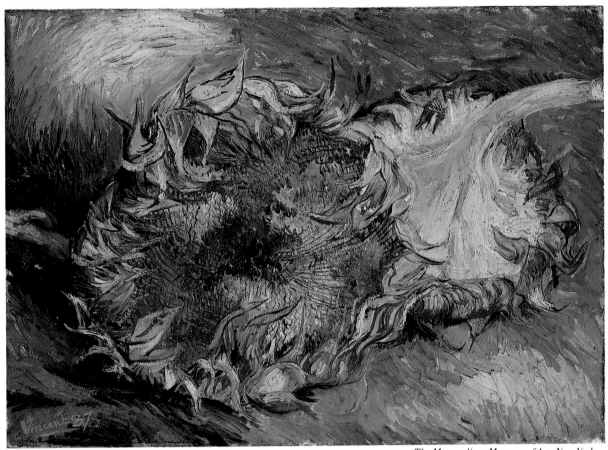

Paris Autumn 1887   oil on canvas
43.2 × 61 (17 × 24)

The Metropolitan Museum of Art New York

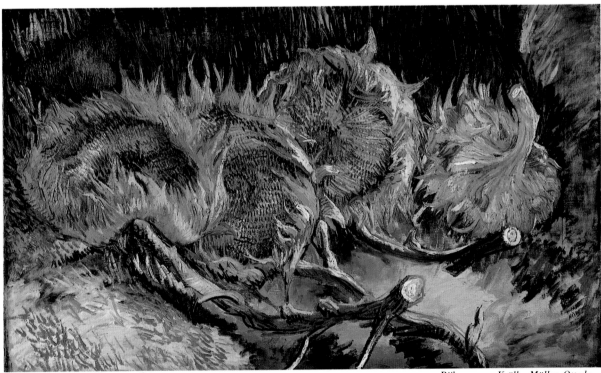

Paris Autumn 1887   oil on canvas
60 × 100 (23⁵/₈ × 39³/₈)

Rijksmuseum Kröller-Müller Otterlo

Earlier, ecstatic over the promised arrival of an almost idolized colleague and while at the crest of his emotional responses as an artist, Van Gogh had painted four canvases of sunflowers to brighten the dreary reality of Gauguin's austere room. Just a handful of blossoms stuck seemingly at random in an old vase. Simple subjects—nothing at all. Nothing except that nothing like them had ever been seen before. Those incandescent still lifes would soon help demolish all barricades separating the established perceptions of art of the past and Van Gogh's "young . . . lovely . . . art of the future" for which he had sacrificed his youth—while painting his eternity.

But that Christmas night, apparently convinced Van Gogh was a hopeless lunatic and dying, Gauguin returned to their house, hastily packed most of his gear and soon left for Paris—two of Vincent's sunflower canvases under his arm. Theo also headed north, probably because he better understood his big brother's inherent Dutch hemp-rope toughness. A few days later, Van Gogh had so fully recovered he visited his studio then returned to the clinic excitedly describing vivid canvases still unpainted in several long letters where he also mixed undiminished admiration for Gauguin with dismay that he had departed Arles so abruptly, taking the sunflower paintings with him. Yet he seemed to accept his loss as the price of friendship with a "genius" but not a saint. With his head still bandaged he then began to copy from memory the looted pictures.

All were nearly identical except for variations in the number of blossoms and background colors. Thanks to Gauguin's sharp eyes and shady character the art world's legacy of Van Gogh sunflower masterpieces grew from four to seven. Though confined to the mental hospital most of the time—which he appeared to accept as just another curious event in his troubled life— he wrote Theo as he started painting again: "Now to get up heat enough to melt that gold, those flower tones, it isn't everybody who can do it, it needs the whole and entire force and concentration of a single individual."

And his destiny with sunflowers was joined forever.

Arles August 1888   oil on canvas
93 × 73 (36 5/8 × 28 3/4)

The National Gallery London
Tate Gallery Loan

Arles August 1888   oil on canvas
91 × 71 (35⁷/₈ × 28)

Neue Pinakothek Munich

Arles January 1889   oil on canvas
100 × 76 (39³/₈ × 30)

Arles January 1889   *oil on canvas*   *The Philadelphia Museum of Art*
$92 \times 72.5 \ (36^{1}/_{4} \times 28^{5}/_{8})$

Arles January 1889   oil on canvas
95 × 73 (37¹/₂ × 28³/₄)

Rijksmuseum Vincent van Gogh Amsterdam

" . . . my pictures are after all
almost a cry of anguish,
although in the rustic sunflower
they may symbolize gratitude"

Vincent writing to Wilhelmina, his sister
Psychiatric ward
Hospital of St. Paul, St. Rémy, France
February, 1890

Photo Data

Every photograph of sunflowers in this book was shot on Kodak VR-400 35mm negative-color film, made for the amateur market. At first, not one of my professional colleagues believed it: photographers, darkroom technicians, art book designers, magazine editors—nobody. Equally unusual—from a former LIFE photographer's point of view—all of the color prints in the book dummy (which I showed around Europe and in the United States when contacting publishers) were made in a one-hour see-it-all shop such as those where most amateurs drop off film after a weekend of swimming, sailing, skiing and snapping away for the family album. The only difference was that the team of young self-trained enthusiasts working with the Noritsu quick-print apparatus in Zurich (whom I met by sheer chance) were masters of their squat monster and demanded results of it, and themselves, that were almost beyond belief—luminous enlargements in twelve minutes for a couple of dollars, remaking any print until I was satisfied. No charge! LIFE's color experts saluted my battered book dummy with respect and now are contemplating adding a quick-printer to their own elaborate darkroom.

There was a compelling motive behind my turning to an amateur's film instead of using Kodachrome or Ektachrome, positive-color emulsions that have recorded everything, everywhere, for decades. The reason was *speed*. Shutter speed, emulsion speed and the speed with which I could develop and check the results of every few days' work. I had very little time. A tripod was too cumbersome, useless. Every shot was hand-held, often at f22 at 1/125th or 1/250th-second for maximum depth-of-field and sharpness, while being buffeted by what Van Gogh called "the devil mistral."

The sunflowers seen here were photographed while driving through the timeless, hauntingly beautiful countryside of France that undulates serenely westward from the Lubéron valley north of Marseilles, skirts the French-Spanish Pyrenees, broadens to include the Loire River Valley, then meets the Atlantic Ocean between La Rochelle and Bordeaux. Sunflowers of course also flourish in Hungary, Spain, Italy and the Soviet Ukraine. Since my interest in them grew from their romantic relationship to Van Gogh and his paintings, I confined my photography to France, beginning in Provence where he created those masterpieces that are so treasured today. And like Van Gogh, I worked at times in the same blinding heat and gale-force mistrals, trying to steady a camera just as he tried to steady his canvases (sometimes lashing them to rocks), until it seemed that my sanity might join his dementia. I loved it. And I imagine he did, too. That summertime battle in the sunflower fields of France was one of the most challenging, and rewarding, experiences of my half-century as a photographer.

All of these pictures are printed full frame and were made with a Nikon FE 35mm camera set on manual-shutter control. My basic lens was a Zoom-Nikkor 35-105mm f3.5, with macro-focusing capability. A Micro-Nikkor 200mm f4 lens was used for many shots *(pages 2, 8, 46–47, 68–69, 70–71, 92–93, 112–113, 114–115, 126–127, 130)*. Each lens was fitted with an L39 filter (ultra-violet) to protect it from dust while also enhancing the richness of many colors. A polarizing filter was often used to emphasize skies and clouds and to subdue some reflections on leaves without eliminating totally the feeling of summer's dazzling sunlight. For other pictures I used a Y44 filter (the most subtle yellow) to add my own interpretations to negatives of subjects where Van Gogh could have slashed on pure pigments wherever desired to alter or exaggerate colors in his canvases.

The advantage of the painter over the photographer.

While shooting this book, I aimed my little four-wheel drive stationwagon down autoroutes, into side roads and sometimes cross-country without benefit of goat paths for 12,500 kilometers (7,500 miles) in the almost-Saharan heat of mid-summer. That's equal to twice across the United States with enough left over to end up in Chicago. It included four roundtrips between the Atlantic Coast of France and Zurich, Switzerland, where I processed my films as often as possible. During that roller-coaster nearly non-stop road rally I had to find and photograph always different combinations of landscapes and sunflowers, while frequently having wild romances with provocative blossoms that cost me dearly in shooting time in other places—still unknown. The entire adventure took twenty-five days, precisely the life-span of a sunflower in full bloom. Then it is finished.

So was I.

"...*it does me good to do difficult things.*
That does not prevent me from having a terrible need of
—shall I say the word?—
of
religion.

"Then I go out at night to paint the stars ..."

DDD